Instant Money Saving Tips for Frugal Living

The Best Ways to Save Money Fast!

Judith Turnbridge

© 2015 Judith Turnbridge

All Rights Reserved. No part of this publication may be reproduced in any form or by any means, including scanning, photocopying, or otherwise without prior written permission of the copyright holder.

Disclaimer and Terms of Use: The Author and Publisher has strived to be as accurate and complete as possible in the creation of this book, notwithstanding the fact that he does not warrant or represent at any time that the contents within are accurate due to the rapidly changing nature of the Internet. While all attempts have been made to verify information provided in this publication, the Author and Publisher assumes no responsibility for errors, omissions, or contrary interpretation of the subject matter herein. Any perceived slights of specific persons, peoples, or organizations are unintentional. In practical advice books, like anything else in life, there are no guarantees of income made. This book is not intended for use as a source of legal, business, accounting or financial advice. All readers are advised to seek services of competent professionals in legal, business, accounting, and finance field.

First Printing, 2015

Printed in the United States of America

Table of Contents

We Must Consult Our Means Rather Than Our Wishes 4

I Want It All and I Want It Now! 5

Distinguishing "Need" From "Want" 6

How to Avoid Impulse Buying 10

Home Tips 14

All About Food 17

Grocery Shopping 22

Easy Budgeting Tips 27

Emergency! Tips to Make Money Fast When You're Completely Broke
.... 43

About the Author 48

We Must Consult Our Means Rather Than Our Wishes

Broke as a joke! Strapped for cash! All tapped out! We've all been there and unfortunately many of us are there now following the recent meltdown in the Global economy. Even with a regular income, bringing up kids, running a busy household, and maintaining a decent standard of living can be a never-ending struggle in this era of rising prices , stagnating wages, and high unemployment rates. All across the country, millions of good, hardworking Americans are feeling the pinch and need to *drastically* tighten their belts; if you're one of them, this book is for you!

Intended as a simple guide for anyone who needs to save money or merely wishes to live more frugally, this book is based upon my personal experiences as a busy, working mom who's lived through the "bad-times." It's also for my family and friends, some of whom were plunged into whirlpools of unmanageable debt and impoverishment following the recent economic crisis.

My goal is to provide a host of simple, common sense ways for saving money. This includes everything from prioritizing your spending to saving on your grocery bill. At the end of the book I'll even give you some emergency ideas for earning money if you have unexpectedly found yourself out of work.

However, before diving into these tips, let's consider *why* you got into financial difficulties in the first place. You may be surprised to find that by just making some small sacrifices, you can actually *improve* the quality of your life rather than ruin it!

I Want It All and I Want It Now!

If you want to know why so many people are crippled by debt, then the aforementioned title of this famous Queen Anthem sums it up nicely; it's not solely due to self-indulgence. However, we've all been actively *encouraged to be greedy!*

For decades, particularly since the 1980s, cheap credit was readily available and material aspirations were heavily promoted. Meanwhile, the cost of living steadily increased and property values soared. Not surprisingly, this encouraged personal debt and a "buy now – pay later" culture. Pretty soon, we were running around in big, expensive cars, living in luxury apartments, and playing with the latest, expensive gadgets that were previously out of our reach. Then the global economic collapse of 2008 exposed the awful truth that we didn't actually own any of it! We were living on someone else's money, and no one knew exactly who the money belonged to in the first place.

So, what lesson can we learn from this history lecture? Forget the credit! Instead, *buy only what you need, when you need it, and only when you can afford it.* Every single tip in this book follows this simple mantra. If you truly live by these guidelines, it'll really change your life.

Distinguishing "Need" From "Want"

You can only follow this mantra successfully, however, if you can distinguish what you actually *need* from what you *want*. Unfortunately, "want" quickly feeds into "need." It is this phenomenon that advertisers mercilessly exploit to increase sales for their clients. Remember when nobody had a computer and the most high-tech thing you had in your purse was lipstick?

Now everyone walks around all day with a laptop or iPad tucked under their arm, blabbing away to their nearest and dearest on a smart phone. Today, in the 21st century, not owning a computerized device is simply unthinkable. It would be like not owning a television, not having an electricity source, or lacking running water in your home. At one time in this country, these things would have been deemed a luxury. In some parts of the world, they still are.

The point is that we can survive on very little indeed. What may seem like a necessity may simply be what we have grown accustomed to as we have gained purchasing power as a society. Always bare this in mind whenever the next must-have gadget appears on the television!

Like everything in life, there are plenty of grey areas here. Some people have a really hard time separating their wants from needs. So for the 99% of us who fail miserably to manage this (Sigmund Fraud made a career from this) here are some points to consider:

Ask Yourself Why You're Buying Stuff in the First Place

Try to make sure you only buy something because it fulfills a basic requirement, not simply because it provides a brief "novelty fix." This may not always be obvious and you need to be strict with yourself about this. Ego and covetousness can also detrimentally sway your purchasing decisions – so be very wary of them. For example, ask yourself if you bought that $500 smart-phone because you really needed it or merely because your neighbor had a cooler model than you!

Think of Retail Therapy as a Disease

When feeling down or bored, many folks will take a trip to the store and buy something "nice" to lift their spirits. This is definitely not a good idea! Building *any* association between the act of spending money and emotional gratification could lead to a full-blown shopping addiction or even financial ruin. It may also mask some deeper psychological issues that need to be addressed.

Instead of buying junk you don't need, why not find cheaper, healthier alternatives for lifting your mood, such as some physical activity or a new hobby. You might even want to consider starting night classes or volunteer work where you can learn new skills, meet new friends, and perhaps even help others less fortunate than yourself.

Be Organized

One *very* effective way of confusing wants with needs is by being poorly organized. If you don't know what you have, how do you know what you need? Often people have so much clutter in their homes they have no idea what they own and constantly waste money by doubling up on stuff.

The answer is to simply clear out the items you don't need and take stock of what's left. In fact, you might just want to read my other Kindle book *"How to Declutter Your Home for Simple Living – Decluttering Tips and Closet Organization Ideas for Creating Your Own Personal Oasis"* because it contains awesome home organization strategies that I've implemented over the years.

Don't Buy Stuff You May Hoard

Before you buy stuff, think about whether or not those items could end up gathering dust in the garage within a couple of months. If the answer is yes, you probably don't *need* it, so then don't bother buying it. Remember, that although you can sell things later, it will usually be at a large loss. Sometimes, however, it is a good idea to make purchases ahead of time, if the items are on sale. That way you'll have it in case it's needed as a future reserve. But, just ensure the item really *is* needed and *will* be used within a few weeks.

Follow the Thirty Day Rule

Now let's move on from hoarding. Whenever you're considering buying something that isn't "essential," wait thirty days and then ask yourself if you still want that item or if it's really worth the cost. This enables you to think logically about the purchase. Quite often, you'll find that the urge to buy has passed during that time, and you'll have saved yourself the money!

Don't Be Penny Wise and Dollar Foolish

A large number of people penny-pinch when they buy silly little things, but splash out carelessly on luxuries they don't need and can't afford. This behavior is so dumb that it drives me, NUTS! What's the sense in spending hours trawling through the mall, attempting to save 10 cents on a bottle of shower gel, only to throw away $100 on some impulsively bought pair of leopard-skin Ugg boots that are worn twice and wind up boxed in the basement gathering dust? Some fools do this sort of thing all the time – just don't be one of them.

Don't Be Penny Foolish and Dollar Wise

Though, a little less annoying than the above, the habit of casually buying the odd little knick- knack, while being sensible about the big-stuff, can be nearly as bad for your wallet! Closely watch EVERYTHING you buy and avoid impulse buying the small things (read on because I cover impulse buying later).

Consider the Unthinkable – Consider Downsizing

Look at the most expensive areas in your life – often these are things you've convinced yourself you cannot live without – and question their necessity. Ask yourself if there are any cheaper or more financially manageable alternatives you could use.

Do you really need a gas-guzzling SUV? Do you even need a car in the first place if you live right next door to a bus station? Do you really need to live in a five-bedroom dream house that's put you into hundreds of thousands of dollars of debt? Maybe you should sell it and go for something less lavish. Maybe you should even settle for a rented accommodation or move to a cheaper area (Oh, the horror! I can hear you crying already!).

I understand. True, these may seem like "nuclear" options and you may not need to go down such drastic routes. However, making sacrifices can have just as many upsides as owning the big stuff in the first place. Oftentimes, the big ticket items can even lead to stress-inducing obligations. For example, owning your own property carries the hassles of securing a mortgage, paying years of interest, maintenance costs, land fees, legal charges (ugh!), etc. You can avoid all of these by renting instead. Though letting go of the car may seem like a dumb idea, you'll never have to worry about tax, insurance costs, losing your "no claims bonus," or finding a parking spot ever again! (If you live in New York City, you'll appreciate the latter point!)

What I'm suggesting is that you question what it is that you actually need in your to life to function effectively as opposed to what might make life a little more exciting. Keep an open mind about the alternatives. You'll be amazed by what you can live without if you make more conscious decisions. So, don't be afraid of the "nuclear" option any longer! Change can be good! Honestly!

Following this theme, having lots of "stuff" (gadgets, jewelry, knick-knacks etc.) may give you a temporary feeling of contentment, but most of it will have become completely worthless, out of fashion, or obsolete in almost the time it has taken you to reach the end of this sentence! Things move so quickly now that today's "object of desire" can become tomorrow's junk almost overnight (we'll cover how best to get rid of it all later – so please read on!).

Having lots of stuff can even invoke "comfort-buying." If you find yourself consistently buried under boxes of redundant garbage like Amiga games, Betamax tapes, grilling machines, and taffeta lampshades, then it's a sign you're buying things in a fruitless attempt to find happiness. Remember, having more stuff won't improve the quality of your life – it'll only clutter it up.

How to Avoid Impulse Buying

Although we've talked about separating want from need and have some idea how to do it, there's still a little spoiled brat in all of us that will almost always make us spend when we shouldn't. And this nasty little brat makes us buy impulsively! As humans, we are wired to impulsively grab at the things we desire. Advertisers and retailers have been exploiting this impulsive behavior for centuries; that's why packaging is so colorful and stores are laid out the way they are.

Unfortunately, impulse buying is addictive! It can cause financial strain, make you fat (if you're forever grabbing candy bars while at the checkout line), and turn your home into a cluttered mess. Therefore, it's crucial that we develop strategies to ward off "Mr. Brat" or "Mrs. Brat" immediately!

Don't Be too Tempted By Sales Pitches

The whole point of sales blurbs is to make you buy impulsively. They exploit our inner bargain hunter through provoking a sense of urgency ("Hurry, While Supplies Last!", "Only Ten Days Left!"), fleeting opportunity, and unparalleled reward ("70% off!", "Buy One – Get One Free!", "Win a vacation!").

Remember though, that something is on sale for *a reason!* It could be because it's simply not selling very well, or maybe it was being sold at an inflated price to begin with. It could even be a "loss-lead," meaning that the item is being sold at a loss in order to entice you to buy more products or to make a little money back on obsolete stock.

The point is to be cynical about sales. Companies are there to make profits – not provide a charitable service. Don't simply purchase something because it appears to be a bargain. Only buy sales items if you actually need them and you're sure you can't get them cheaper anywhere else.

Follow the Thirty Day Rule

As I mentioned earlier, give yourself thirty days to think about your non-essential purchases before making them. This allows time for your head to rule your heart!

Try to Shop Online

Buying from the Web helps you to avoid temptation from all the marketing tricks the stores employ to get you to part with your hard-earned cash (sales, special offers, deals, tuneless guitar players, men in funny costumes, etc.). Moreover, goods can often be bought far more cheaply online than in a store. So, it's good practice to try this first before venturing to the mall.

It's also a good idea to install a free pop-up blocker when browsing sites like YouTube (AdBlock Plus works great for this and can be easily installed for free by visiting adblockplus.org), in order to stop bad influences from directed ads. There's much more about online shopping later.

Don't Go to the Store too Often

The more you go, the more you'll leave yourself open to temptation. Limit your visits to a maximum of once or twice a week.

Try to Shop Alone

Though a trip to the store can be fun, you should always focus on the business at hand. Unless they are like-minded, shopping with friends will always bring out the compulsive spender in you. (I can hear it now; "Jude, those shoes look great with that dress – oh, those earrings are just too gorgeous too – you gotta' get em' all girl – you deserve it!" blah, blah, blah…). Likewise, if you're lucky enough to have a babysitter, leave the kids at home to avoid their dreaded "pester power" too!

Never Make a Purchase You Cannot Return

Sometimes, particularly when buying gifts, you may find that you've made an unnecessary purchase or that an item doesn't work properly. Therefore, always make sure that any store you buy from has a friendly return policy. This will help you to avoid wasting money as well as collecting unwanted junk!

Only Carry a Limited Amount of Cash With You at All Times

Leaving home without your credit cards may seem like casting out onto a stormy sea without wearing a life preserver. But think about it. If you don't have the dough on you then you won't be able to spend it or waste it on frivolous purchases! Take the bare minimum of cash that you may need with you and leave your bankcards, credit cards, and checkbooks where they belong – at home!

Embracing this limitation will make it much tougher for you to buy impulsively and it also allows you to stick to your budget more effectively. In fact, research shows that the average American shopper will spend between 10-35% less per year if they regularly pay in cash, rather though bank or credit cards. In some cases, you may even be able to get the occasional good deal if you offer to pay cash up front, particularly for electronic gadgets in some of the smaller independent stores.

Never Go Shopping While You're Hungry

Grab a bite to eat before you embark on a shopping trip! This will help you avoid having your stomach influencing your purchasing decisions by enticing you to buy worthless snacks. It's amazing how much more inviting food looks and smells on the shelves, even when you're only slightly hungry.

Keep Your Distance

Unless buying fresh vegetables, try to avoid touching the items as you browse the store's shelves. Studies have shown that the physical act of picking up an item while you shop encourages you to buy it because it builds a psychological association between that object and your ownership of it.

Avoid Whatever Triggers Your Spending

By "triggers," I mean any situation where you might be tempted to automatically overspend without a second thought. This might include going out with friends to a restaurant or bar, throwing a dinner party, or especially when vacationing with the kids! (Has anyone ever heard of a *cheap* theme park? I didn't think so!)

Only Go Down the Aisles When You Must

While shopping, don't wander down an aisle unless you have to. This will help you avoid any temptations. If you don't see it, then you won't even know what you're missing. Simple!

Avoid Sampling Food, Unless It's Already on Your List

Sample foods are there to tempt you to try the food and like it so that you end up making an unplanned purchase. Steer clear of those sample ladies unless you actually need what they are offering.

Home Tips

This section covers the topic of how to avoid spending money on your home, and even how to supplement your income from it.

Rent It

If you have a spare room, rent it out. If you have one that is under used, clear out the stuff you don't need, put what's left into another room, and rent it out. However, try not to become so dependent on your rental income that you need it to stay afloat.

Sometimes things go wrong and you can find yourself stuck with a bad tenant. You'll have to put up with them longer than you should while frantically searching for another and you may be forced to take on the next without checking them out properly. Often this can lead to a vicious circle of bad tenants, not to mention the panic you will feel every time you need to find a replacement. For this reason, it's a good idea to offer short-term contacts with easy-to-break clauses.

When taking on a tenant, ask yourself if they can be of any use to you. *Are they good at plumbing? Can they decorate? Do they work in the childcare field?* Sometimes they will work for you for a temporary reduction in rent or a cut in utility bills. They may even work for an upgrade to their "pad," such as a bigger dresser, a better washing machine, or the installation of a dedicated broadband TV package. Moreover, they tend to do a better job when working on the premises where they live.

Keep It Maintained

Regularly, go around your home and do a little light maintenance and grounds work. Even if you aim for an hour, once a month, it'll make a huge difference. If you're proactive instead of reactive, you can avoid paying out hefty bills in the future on professional repairs when something breaks that could've been easily maintained.

If you're not sure how to fix something, grab a handyman book from your local library or search the Internet for tips. If you have a friend or family member who is handy, call in a favor. There are also plenty of home repair videos out there, especially on YouTube!

Get a Smaller Place

I mentioned previously about downsizing, but there are even more benefits to this than I discussed earlier. So, let's investigate them further!

First of all, you'll have a smaller mortgage. People forget that the interest payments, when added together, can come to much more than the value of the property. By downsizing, you'll not only save each month, you'll also save a ton of money long term.

Some people are tempted to get a bigger mortgage by the Mortgage Interest Tax Break. However, this in no-way offsets the overall interest you'll be ultimately charged on your home. This scheme is under fire and may be scrapped altogether under proposed reforms.

If you're lucky, and you've paid off much of your mortgage, downsizing could leave you with a nice little "nest egg" for your retirement!

Smaller places also have less operating costs. They are easier and cheaper to maintain, service, heat, keep clean, furnish, and carpet. They also invariably have lower ground rates. (I'm getting tempted to move myself after writing this!). As you can see, downsizing has *a lot* of benefits!

Don't Be Lazy – Do It Yourself

Unless you have a chronic injury, mow the lawn, do the gardening, wash the car, sweep the courtyard, walk the dog, and do other typical chores all by your little, old self! It's astonishing how many people pay a bunch of pimply kids to do these simple everyday tasks. Doing these physical activities is also great for keeping fit (as long as you don't have a major back problem!).

If your place already looks particularly immaculate, maybe you could even offer similar services to your neighbors for some extra cash or a "service exchange."

You can save even more money if you grow your own herbs, berries, fruits, and vegetables. If you have a particularly "green thumb," or make a nifty blueberry preserve, you might be able to make a little cash by selling your excess produce at local farmer's markets or to an independent retailer. Many cottage industries that produce "artisan" foods cut their teeth selling stuff that was grown in the owner's backyard!

All About Food

Food is one of the biggest drains on anyone's budget, particularly if they have a family to feed. So, here are a few quick and useful tips for you to consider.

Go on a Diet

Yep, it's as simple as that! This may sound obvious, but America, like the rest of the Western world, is going through an obesity epidemic. We are all eating far too much and not exercising enough, which has serious consequences for everyone's well-being. By getting used to eating smaller portions, not only will you save your wealth, you may even save your health! (Get it?)

Budget Your Food Bill

Set a dollar limit on how much you want to spend on groceries each week and stick to it! This will force you to think about what you are buying.

Only Eat Out or Get Takeout on Special Occasions

Buying takeout food or eating at fast food chains and restaurants are great ways of paying overpriced prices for your meals. Cook at home instead!

Learn to Cook From Scratch

Look, if I can do it, *anyone* can! Invest in night school cooking classes if you need to because home cooking is *by far* the cheapest way of feeding yourself and the family. And by cooking, I don't mean merely putting ready-made meals into the microwave oven. Ready-made meals have small portions, can be unhealthy, are usually over-priced, and often taste horrible. The same applies for pre-prepared sauces. So, grab that apron, fire up the stove, and impress your family with a homemade meal, cooked from scratch!

Use the Web to Find Recipes

Nowadays, because of the wonders of the Internet, there are literally thousands of free recipes out there, even if you're budget-conscious. Collect the best and exchange them with your family and friends!

Cook Food in Batches

Cooking foods like soups, stews, casseroles, and stir-fries in batches saves time and money on energy costs. Cook large amounts of these foods and divide them into individual meal-sized portions. Then schedule when to use them and store them in the freezer.

Buy a Crock-Pot

You will need something to use for your batch cooking, now won't you? A good sized crock-pot is a very cost-effective, fuss-free tool for cooking delicious meals for the entire family.

Get a Big Freezer

Invest in a nice, big, freezer. You can either get a good secondhand one or a brand new one if you can afford it. This will allow you to buy and store freezable sale items in bulk, as well as freeze batches of cooked food. Keep your freezer appropriately stocked to keep its temperature stable and save on energy bills.

Use Leftovers

Don't waste anything! Save all your leftovers and prepare new meals with them. There are thousands of recipes out there to help you with this, so open that browser, and start looking!

Buy Food Items You Can Use in Many Ways

Foods, such as milk, eggs, pasta, bread, pulses, rice, canned vegetables, beans, ground meat, etc. are cheap and easy to store. Always buy these items in bulk. You'll then be able to provide a bewildering array of healthy, wholesome meals.

Use Meat as a Treat

Americans love big hunks of juicy steak or massive piles of chicken wings and ribs. For most of us, the meat makes up the bulk of our meals. However, in many cultures meat is viewed almost like a condiment. Just think of Asian food and you'll see what I mean. Meat is easily the most expensive part of a meal. If you cut back on the meat, not only will you be healthier, you'll be richer too. Likewise, why not go vegetarian occasionally!

Meat prices tend to fluctuate wildly, so when they are high, a vegetarian meal, using mushrooms, eggs, or beans for protein will be a *much* cheaper alternative. If you have any bacon rinds, bones, or meat cuttings left over, don't throw them away or feed them to the dog. Instead, boil them up into a delicious meaty stock or soup.

Remember That We Eat With Our Eyes

We are programmed to think that the greater the number of things we see, the more there is in mass. For example, by serving two thin slices of meat, instead of one thick slice, you'll be fooling your diners into thinking they are actually getting more food! It works! Trust me! Another trick is to serve food on smaller plates. It has exactly the same effect!

Choose Fruits and Vegetables That Are In-Season

Fruit and vegetables are more expensive out of season. They also lack flavor. So, build your menus around what's fresh and cheap (always check over any produce on the clearance table in case they are beginning to go bad).

Freeze Those Fruits and Veggies

During the summer, freeze or can your cheap in-season fruit and vegetables for the winter.

Avoid Ready-To-Cook Mixes

Store-bought cake, cookies, and pancake mixes are never as good as homemade. Plus, they are really expensive! So why not have a bash making your own?

Say Goodbye to Fancy Desserts

I don't just mean the posh stuff like a gateaux or cream pie. I mean the humble stuff like doughnuts, waffles, and even bars of chocolate. Not only are these of dubious nutritional value, they are fattening and very expensive too!

Fill That Oven

If they all need similar baking times, fill your oven with more than one item. Don't overcrowd it though, and don't be tempted to add stuff during baking. If you open the oven while it's cooking, you may let out the heat and ruin the meal.

Buy Day-Old Bread

Day-old bread, or loaves on special are fine to eat and are much cheaper than buying fresh. If you keep bread in the freezer, it will last much longer. You can keep it in the fridge as well, but just make sure the loaf is thoroughly wrapped in cling wrap to avoid it drying out too quickly.
Remember to save the crusts and ends. If you toast them in the oven, then crush them up, they make excellent breadcrumbs! Don't throw away stale bread or feed it to the birds (it's much too good for them!). Stale bread actually makes much better toast than fresh!

Take a Lunch Packed at Home

Homemade sandwiches are much cheaper than store bought and you know what's in them! Many store-prepared sandwiches are chock full of salt, fat, and preservatives. That's makes them hardly a "healthy" option for lunch. Those leftovers that I talked about before can also make a great lunch. That'll also keep you from being tempted to eat out for lunch.

Avoid Vending Machines

If you want to spend double on the same snack you could buy for much less in the store, then go ahead and waste your money! You shouldn't be snacking anyway if you're trying to cut costs, but if you do, never buy from a vending machine – they're a rip-off!

Entertain at Home Instead of Going Out

Take turns hosting dinner parties with your friends. Entertain with pot roast or cheap buffets to keep the costs down.

Regularly Check Use-By Dates

Each week, check the contents of your fridge, freezer, and kitchen cabinets for anything that's about to go past its use-by date. If you find anything ready to expire, don't throw it away! Use it up immediately!

Grocery Shopping

Make a List and Stick to It

Plan your meals, make a shopping list, and stick to it like glue! If it's not on the list, don't buy it unless it's a *really, really* good deal (i.e. double coupon offers).

Before making a list, always look through the contents of your freezer, kitchen cabinets, and pantry to figure out what you need, as well as to avoid making duplicate purchases.

Finally, as you get to the checkout, weed-out any items in your shopping basket that are not on the list or not needed.

Check for Offers and Coupons Before Going Shopping

Before leaving for the store, quickly scour the local newspapers for sales. Grabs some scissors and cut out any coupons or vouchers you may find. Check out the website of your grocery store for other special deals.

If the offers *really* are "good ones," build your meals around them. Make sure, however, that you only buy sale items if you really *need them* and not because you can get them cheap!

Only Buy Food at the Grocery Store

Often you can get toiletries, cosmetics, electrical goods, and more for a whole lot cheaper someplace other than the grocery store.

Shop at Discount Stores

Discount stores are actually cheaper than buying with coupons from big supermarkets, and they are way cheaper than convenience stores. Convenience stores are often grossly overpriced and should be avoided like the plague!

Bring a Calculator

Not only can you keep a running total as you shop, it's also great for figuring out unit prices when they're not listed.

Keep a Notebook Handy

Jot down the normal prices of the things you regularly buy, so you can keep track of trends and recognize small price changes.

Buy Loose Veggies, But Always Check the Price

Multi-pack bags or trays of vegetables are traditionally much more expensive to buy than those sold individually. (The opposite is true of canned food, however). Many people know this and so they automatically go for the cheaper "loose" stuff. Unfortunately, the more unscrupulous stores exploit this expectation by raising the price of individually sold items to match the multi-pack bags. Therefore, you should never take anything for granted; always compare the price-per item between packed and loose items before you buy.

Shop Early and Give Yourself Plenty of Time

Going through the store before it becomes crowded ensures there are still bargains to be had and allows you the chance to take your time and properly scrutinize what's available. Hopefully, you will find fully stocked shelves early in the morning and get those sale items before they sell out.

Avoid Sliced and Diced Foods

Pre-cut foods, like chopped vegetables (NOT canned) and chunked meat may be convenient, but they cost a fortune compared to the un-chopped stuff. Grab a knife, learn to use it, and chop-it-up yourself.

Buy Chunked Canned Stuff

Cans of chopped fruits and veggies tend to be cheaper than un-chopped; i.e. chopped tomatoes and pineapples will cost less than plum tomatoes and pineapple rings.

Buy Generic Brands

Don't be tempted into thinking the expensive brand-named items are better than the generic. Often, generic goods are made by the same manufacturers as the "good" stuff. In fact, in some cases they may even contain the exact same product just in different packaging!

Compare Food Prices in Different Forms

Compare the cost of a food against its frozen, dried, or canned forms and go for the cheapest one. Obviously, consider the quality of what you buy (frozen peas, for example, are slightly more expensive than canned, but are about a thousand times more palatable than those canned peas that are almost inedible).

Avoid Single Servings

Single servings of items such as crackers, juice, or ice cream are way overpriced and certainly not worth the poor value. Avoid them at all costs!

Look at the Top and Bottom Shelves

Grocers usually put the items they want to sell at eye level and within easy reach. The better values are often put out-of-the-way on the top or bottom shelves. Sometimes, you'll even have to dig to the back of a shelf before finding the item you are looking for. Therefore, it's a good idea to rummage around the shelves to dig out those bargains!

Double-Check Your Receipt

Sometimes special deals are not correctly programmed into the checkout system (especially those self-service machines). Always check your receipts for errors. Use itemized receipts to keep track of your purchases if you are able to do so. You can easily keep yourself from paying more than you have to by implementing this simple tip.

Be Wary of the Clearance Section

Although it's always worth checking out, clearance items are often those that were more expensive to begin with. You can probably get a fresher version of the item for less. Also avoid dented cans as the contents may be damaged.

Figure Out When the Store Restocks

Usually, grocery stores restock their shelves once a week and mark-down the items that aren't selling. Be brave and ask the staff when they restock and shop only on those days. You may pick up some awesome bargains!

Shop Around

Always keep an open mind when shopping. Never assume a certain grocery chain will always be cheaper than another. Periodically, check out the competition – you might be surprised by what you find. Remember to factor in the cost of transportation when shopping around or you may end up wasting any savings on gas or fares!

Buy the Essentials in Bulk

Buying in bulk is always cheaper, so stock up on essential groceries that can be used in a variety of ways. Also, bulk-buy when the cost-per-item decreases significantly (i.e. > 5%), but (obviously) avoid the stuff that can go bad quickly! Consider splitting your bulk-buying costs with a friend, so you'll both save cash!

Buy Lean Meat in Family Packs

Lean meat is not only better for you, but it's a better value too! By buying lean meat, you'll avoid paying for all the unwanted fat or bone you'll find on chops, ribs, or non-lean cuts since meat is sold by the pound. If you buy in family packs, you'll find even greater savings. Just freeze it and consume it as needed.

Buy Cheaper Cuts of Meat

Though we all love a juicy T-bone steak, there are many cheaper cuts of meat that are just as tasty and satisfying if prepared correctly. Try slow roasted pork belly, for instance, or maybe even offal. Though some may flinch at the thought of eating kidneys, liver, and other organs, offal has long been considered by many top-chefs as premium food – and it's very good for you, too!

Get Friendly With the Butcher

Often the butcher will point out the best value cuts for customers. So get on his good side and get advice from the expert. Sometimes you can even get great tips on how to prepare and cook your meat purchases.

Don't Buy Ice Cubes

You have an ice tray in your freezer, don't you? Use that instead of paying for frozen water!

Avoid Bottled Water

Tap water in the United States is pretty good, on the whole. So, why buy the overpriced bottled stuff? If you're that silly (or fussy), maybe buy a water filter instead.

Easy Budgeting Tips

This section is comprised of all those little tips that can't be neatly categorized, but are applicable to nearly every situation. You'll find some of the best tips you'll ever need right here.

Kill That Credit Card

Get out of the mindset that credit is cool – it isn't! Credit simply allows you to live beyond your means and fall into the trap of debt. A few years back, the advice would have been to simply avoid credit cards or loans altogether. My mom used to say that once you'd paid off your credit card debt, the first thing you should do was grab a pair of scissors and cut up that card into little pieces!

Nowadays, because of the Internet we often have no option but to pay by credit card. If you're forced to pay with a card, use a debit card if you can. However, if you do pay with a credit card, make sure you pay it off as quickly as possible to avoid those horrible interest charges!

Check Your Statements

We all make mistakes and big companies are no exception! Always check your bank statements and utility bills carefully each month to look for errors!

Try to Borrow It

Why spend money when you can borrow something instead? People you know can certainly help you out by lending you something that they have and that you need.

Obviously, it's important to take care of whatever you borrow and return the item to its owner as soon you're finished with it. Always return an item in at least as good a state as it was when you borrowed it. (i.e. clean it up!).

Borrowing items from family, friends, and neighbors is also a great way to try something out before you buy it. It certainly helps you to avoid costly purchasing mistakes! It's also a nice idea to offer to lend something of yours back to a person who lent you something, if you can.

Try to Mend and Make Do

Before buying replacement stuff, consider the following useful tips:

1) Clean It Up

Sometimes even the most tired-looking, worn out item can be given a new lease of life with just a little cleaning. Recently I found some ancient, crusty-looking cooking utensils buried in an old dusty box in my parents attic. I polished them up with a little baking soda and lemon juice and within minutes they were as good as new!

You don't even need to buy any harmful and expensive cleaning products to do the job. In many cases homemade, non-toxic preparations can work just as well and maybe even better! (For more economical cleaning tips, why not check out another one of my Kindle books: *Super Simple Home Cleaning – The Best House Cleaning Tips for Green Cleaning the Home*, which is available on Amazon).

2) Upgrade It

I don't just mean upgrading the obvious – like computers (I'm a real technophobe, but even I acknowledge some upgrades are really easy to do on these, like attaching external hard-drives or even adding more memory, if you're feeling particularly brave).

Upgrading in this case covers anything that can be improved with just a little know-how, time, and effort. For instance, you could upgrade your home with a little redecorating or a coat of paint. You can even do something more ambitious like putting in a walk-in closet or a new kitchen.

Think about upgrading an old piece of clothing with a little judicious sewing or dyeing. You can even upgrade an old toy by sitting down with your kids and letting them loose at it with some water-based paint in the yard! The list is endless! Just make sure that for anything technical, you are competent enough to do the upgrade without breaking anything. Also, keep in mind to only do upgrades that are *really* needed, not just being done on a whim!

3) Fix It Yourself

Obviously, if you attempt to fix something without knowing what you're doing, you can make things a whole lot worse. Botched repairs by amateurs can be dangerous and could even lead to the need for expensive professional repairs later on!

I had one numbskull neighbor who was so tight with money he tried to "fix" his broken step ladder by wrapping the handles in gardening twine (a prime example of *penny wise and dollar foolish* as discussed earlier in this book). Needless to say, he wound up in the hospital with a fractured pelvis after trying to adjust his outdoor TV antenna.

But if you know you won't kill anyone and you're not going to wind up with a $1000 bill if it all goes wrong, try fixing things yourself. If it's broken anyway, what do you have to lose? If you do manage to fix it, not only have you saved money by not buying a replacement, you'll undoubtedly feel very pleased with yourself. You might even learn a new skill along the way!

4) Make Do With What You've Got

Sometimes people replace things unnecessarily because they've become accustomed to having them, rather than actually needing them. I'm guilty of this myself. Recently I'd gotten used to using an expensive battery powered can opener shaped like an egg that would run on its own accord around the rim of the can as it cut off the lid. It was almost useless. The thing was forever falling off and when it did work, it left a nasty razor-sharp edge on the top of the can.

I'd gotten so used to using it, however, that I rushed out to get another when it broke. When I couldn't find one at my local store, I ordered it online. While waiting for its delivery, I used an old handheld opener instead and it worked so much better than the electric model! I ended up canceling my order and continuing to use the old one.

So, the moral of this story is: before you replace an item, check to see if you've already got something that will do the same job.

5) Do Without It Completely

Sometimes we get accustomed to doing tasks that are completely unnecessary and then we waste money buying things related to those tasks. If you find you're not missing an item once it has broken, it's probably not required anymore so it shouldn't be replaced.

Follow the Five Question Rule

Let's say you've picked up an item, gotten out your purse or wallet, and are about to make your way to the checkout. Don't do it! Stop, take a deep breath, and ask yourself the following five questions. If your answer is "yes" to any of them, put it back and forget about buying it!

1) Can I Find It Cheaper?

If you're not sure, assume you can. Never ever buy an item unless you *know* you're getting a good deal!

2) Do I Already Have Something Like It at Home?

If so, there's little point in buying it now, right?

3) Is There Anything Wrong With It?

Be *very* critical. Assess the item to see if it's awkward to use, scratched, or damaged in any way. Does it look poorly made? Does it seem safe? (i.e. can the kids use it without harming themselves?)

4) Is There a Chance I'll Never Use the Item or May Tire of It Quickly?

Often, when in the midst of impulse buying, we'll make up all kinds of foolish reasons for purchasing something that looks really stupid in "the cold light of day." So, another way of posing this question is *"Am I about to buy something I'll regret?"*

5) Is It Worth It?

This is actually a very personal issue; what may seem like a bargain to one person may seem like a rip-off to another. The value you place on an item may even vary from day to day (hence the thirty day rule I mentioned earlier). So, ask yourself how that item will benefit your life and then weigh that assessment against the sacrifices you'll need to make after purchasing it. Those sacrifices could be trivial, but they could also be huge. (Buying a 30 cent candy bar won't "break the bank," but purchasing a $30,000 speedboat would be a very different proposition!)

Also, when comparing different models of the same item, think about whether or not the added cost of the more expensive versions truly reflect their alleged superiority over the cheaper models. For instance, does spending an extra $100 on a "limited-edition" mobile phone with a pretty cover really make it work any better? Will dishing out another $1000 on the "exhaust-tuning kit" for your car really turn it into a Ferrari? It might make it sound like one, but it surely won't make it drive like one. (This author's son should take note!)

Consider Renting

Renting or leasing cars, mobile phones, TV's, etc. can be a great way of keeping your costs down and can lead to cheaper upgrade paths for you in the future. Moreover, if anything happens to go wrong with your rented stuff, it is usually replaced or repaired free of charge. Most importantly, if you run into financial difficulties, you can easily rid yourself of the burden of paying for them by canceling your contracts. This is a far better option for saving money than selling off your stuff at a loss, pawning your treasured belongings, or defaulting on your credit card payments!

Consider Buying Secondhand Goods

You'll be absolutely amazed what you can get for next to nothing, when you buy items secondhand – TVs, stereos, books, designer clothing, and even automobiles. One extreme example is that I have a musician friend who purchases cars for $100, runs them into the ground, and then sells them for parts or scrap. When he's finished with them, he'll simply buy another old clunker with the money he's made. His current car is a 20-year-old Toyota that he's owned for three straight years without breakdown and it cost him next to nothing!

Obviously you need to know what to look for to avoid buying a heap of junk that breaks down within a week, but there are some truly astonishing bargains out there if you look for them. Moreover, things can only improve in the secondhand market. Since the 1990s, cars tend to be better made with galvanized steel, so they last much longer. If you're not into driving around in a cruddy old car, like my musician friend, go for vehicles labeled "late model used." These cars typically come straight from a lease, which means reliable owners probably did a nice job caring for them. However, always check the paperwork and thoroughly scrutinize the service history. If these raise any doubts – don't buy the car!

Feel embarrassed about riding around in a secondhand vehicle? Don't be. Firstly, if *you* don't care, why should you care what *others* think? That's their problem, not yours! Secondly, if you get it right, you'll have WAY more money left in your pocket than they'll have after buying a fancy new car!

Buy Refurbished Goods

A great way to get hold of a bargain is to buy warranted stock that's been refurbished. This is especially applicable for techie goods, like mobile phones, computer monitors, TVs, mp3 players, and other such items. Don't purchase them unless they come with a warrantee, however. Obviously, like all secondhand gear, refurbished items stand a greater chance of breaking down than new stuff and Murphy's Law dictates that if you buy *anything* without a warrantee, something will go wrong the first time you use it!

But keep in mind that there's no point in having any type of warranty if you lose the paperwork. Be sure to save all the receipts for your larger purchases in a special folder and lock that away in a filing cabinet. Alternatively, it's a great idea to keep your "receipts folder" in some sort of fire-retardant safe. Apart from protecting them from the obvious, this will keep the paperwork from getting damp from condensation, as well as indicate their importance. Domestic safes tend to be quite small inside too, so you won't be tempted to cram it with all sorts of irrelevant junk the way you can with a filing cabinet.

Beware of Gimmicks Regarding Warranties

While having a standard warranty is essential, extended warranties are often a waste of time and money. Though these may seem like a good idea at first, many items become obsolete way before the extension period kicks in. So, there's a good chance you'd have replaced them long before then! In addition, don't forget to read the fine print. Besides being overpriced, many warranties contain all sorts of "get-out" clauses for the seller.

The same is true for other "gimmicks" like leases, add-ons, etc. because just like extended warranties, they are simply ways for companies to get more money from you.

Check Out the Thrift Stores

You can buy some amazing stuff at charity outlet stores. Not only may you find a bargain or two, you'll be helping those who are much less fortunate than you.

A great tip is to check out the thrift stores in affluent areas, as they tend to sell higher quality gear that is often hardly used. My shrewd husband recently spotted a pair of stout working boots in a thrift shop. He has really big feet and has trouble finding shoes that fit him, so he's always looking out for some. Just by coincidence, he spotted the boots in the shop window and went in to look at them. The soles were perfect, the leather was immaculately clean, they were already polished, and the only sign of ware was nothing more than a couple of small scuffmarks on the toecap. Later we found out they were initially from Sears, cost about $160 new, and he got them for just 40! They fit great and look great – a real bargain!

Worried about wearing secondhand gear? Don't be! All thrift shops have a "public-hygiene" policy, so they aren't permitted to sell dirty clothing. If you're still concerned, simply give them a thorough wash before you wear them. Some thrift stores are so health-conscious that they won't even sell secondhand books. That's pretty ironic considering how many hands touch the books that you can check out from the public library!

If you still feel "cheap" wearing donated items, try to focus on finding a bargain and take pride in yourself for saving money. If you're still hung-up about it, keep quiet – nobody is going to know it's secondhand unless you tell them!

Checkout the Discount Stores

Take a regular trip to your local "no-frills" discount store and buy any regularly used essentials, like toilet paper, paper towels, laundry detergent, dish soap, etc. in bulk. Keep an eye out for any special deals or coupons. But only do this if – and only if – they include items you had already intended to purchase. As I've stated before, don't be tempted to buy something just because it's on sale; buy only the items you need.

Always Buy the Best You Can Afford for Your Biggest Purchases

This may seem a little contradictory – one minute I'm blabbing on about buying secondhand goods and the next I'm saying "only buy the best," but the key words here are ***best*** and ***afford***. It's all a question of how well you expect an item to perform and for how long you expect to keep it. If you buy something new and cheap, it will almost certainly be of lower design quality than an equivalently-priced secondhand item. The used item will probably not work anywhere near as well or for as long as a brand-new, more expensive model.

Here's a personal example: When we moved into our first apartment, my "audiophile" husband blew a cool $1000 on a very high-end hi-fi separates system – I could have killed him! Fortunately, it turned out to be a very wise choice. He spent weeks researching and listening to different systems before he settled on what one to get. Then he spent another couple of weeks shopping around and haggling with sales associates for the best price. But believe it or not, that system is still going strong! It works superbly and we still use it every day to listen to our vinyl collection – and *it's over thirty years old! That comes to less than 30 dollars per year!* Moreover, many components from it are highly prized by collectors and have virtually held their price after all this time.

This example illustrates what I mean when I say buy the *"best" – it works well for a long time.* But there is another point to mention here – we could *afford* it. *We did not have to make any real sacrifices or go into debt over this purchase.* My husband was starting to make a decent wage and we *paid for it out of his savings*, not our joint account. He also considered the fact that he could most likely sell it for a good price if he had to. I rest my case!

Buy Stuff You Could Make Money On

One thing to note from the previous example is that my hubby deliberately chose items that he thought would have a good resale value. This is a great habit to get into and it doesn't just apply to the obvious stuff like houses, cars, furniture, jewelry, and collectibles. For instance, buying a decent business suit may land you a better job. Furthermore, providing a double bed for your spare room will make it more attractive to lodgers. As they say in business: sometimes you need to speculate to accumulate!

There is one exception, however; unless you're an expert and can afford to take the occasional loss, never-never-never buy anything you *think* will be an investment if you don't need it or may not use it. This is one of the easiest ways I know of throwing your money down the drain and transforming your home into a junkyard!

Take Care of Your Belongings

Moving on from that last point, make sure you take proper care of your belongings. Read the manufacturers care instructions and when required, get your item regularly and professionally serviced. At the very least, keep it clean! Not only will the condition of an item directly affect its resale value, well-maintained items tend to last much longer too!

Don't Wait Until It's Too Late

If something is starting to show signs that it's about to go *kaput*, never wait until the item has totally broken down before you replace it. This is especially applicable for essential items such as cars, washing machines, atomic power stations, and the like. Give yourself time to make alternative arrangements, properly research a replacement, and find a good deal.

Think of the Future

Not only does thinking ahead apply to your existing items, it's always a good idea to keep an eye out for independent reviews and special deals when planning to purchase new stuff.

Therefore, you should always take some time to consider all the things you may need to purchase in the future. Avoid the temptation to buy something simply because it's easy or convenient to get hold of – do your homework and always buy the best for the price you can afford.

Buy Stuff at the End of the Season

By buying Christmas items immediately after Christmas, winter clothes just as the spring collections appear, or summer gear when the autumn season starts, you will literally save yourself a fortune! I tend to buy many of my Christmas and birthday presents on December 27 and give them to my loved ones throughout the following year. That way I have the choice of saving money or giving bigger gifts for the amount I would have spent pre-season. Obviously, the kids will ask for special presents for Christmas, and it's a bit mean to expect them to wait all year for them, so these will need to be bought ad-hoc. However, if you're lucky enough to have a child born close to the festive season, give them one of their requested items Christmas morning. Then, buy the rest when they go on sale and give those out on their birthday.

Buying off-season is especially useful when purchasing celebratory cards for Mother's Day, Father's Day etc., as the same designs are often recycled endlessly in the shops and never go out-of-date. Buy these cards immediately after the day concerned and give them out over the coming year.

Don't Be a Fashion Victim

I know it's hard, particularly for the young, not to be swayed by the latest fads in fashion. But, there are certain styles that are constantly recycled and that'll never look dated. For example, the "little black dress" or the "navy blue suit" will never go out of style. The majority of your clothes should be classic pieces and then you can use various fashion accessories to keep up with the trends.

Pay for Things by Offering Your Services

If you have any practical skills, offer your services as payment. My husband is a whiz at accounting and I'm a pretty good bookkeeper as well. Therefore, we often offer to do the books for the tradespeople we use in exchange for a discount on the work they do for us. We also swap services with neighbors and friends. By doing this, we often get things done for nothing more than a little bit of time!

Avoid Being a Gadget Freak

Some idiots – sorry, I mean people – rush out and buy the very latest must-have gadgets, just out of novelty. Apart from buying stuff they don't need, they are also encouraging dependency on them later on (remember – "want" feeds into "need"). Moreover, earlier versions of any new technology are guaranteed to be buggy and of poor value compared to later models as prices drop and features improve.

A classic example is the pocket calculator. These calculators cost around $300 – $500 when they first appeared in the early 1970s. They were power-hungry, bulky, LED beasts that did comparatively little; some even had really weird quirks to them. Calculators were the space age marvels of the day. Within a few short years, however, you could buy vastly better models for less than a tenth of the price of the originals. There are many more recent examples too. Think about PC's, mobile phones, and game consoles in particular.

In addition, take into consideration that standards are often not set when new technologies are introduced to the market. Remember Betamax? This videotape format was supposedly far superior to the VHS alternative, but it never quite caught on and very few feature films were available in that format. When launched, Betamax VCRs appeared to be the natural purchasing choice, but within a couple of years they were literally worthless. So, the point is to not rush out and buy new technology when it first appears. Instead, wait at least a couple of years when prices drop and you can see how things are panning out.

Don't Be Afraid to Ask for Discounts

All businesses are desperate to keep you as a customer and you'll be amazed just how amenable they can be if you ask for a discount. This is particularly applicable to cable and satellite TV companies, utility providers, and the mobile phone networks. Let's put it this way: they certainly aren't going to cut off your services if you try! What do you have to lose?

Don't Be Afraid to Haggle

As a rule, most companies would rather sell their stuff for less profit rather than not selling anything at all. So, why not indulge in some bartering? You'll be stunned by what you can save when you haggle, especially when buying electronic goods from independent retailers. If they won't offer you a discount, ask for coupons or get them to throw in something extra for free (make sure you *really* want what they offer though – personally I'd aim to get the original item cheaper rather than be offered a bunch of freebies). If you're not used to haggling, it may seem a little daunting at first, but you'll quickly get the hang of it. And I guarantee you'll grow to love it!

Give Up Smoking and Any Other Expensive Habits You Might Have

Imagine what life would be like if you had a tax-free, pay raise of over $2,000 per year. Now what if all you had to do to get it was to stop doing something *really stupid*.

In fact, this should've been tip number one! Stop smoking. Period. If you smoke, you know how expensive it is and, unless you've been living on the Moon for the past 60 years, you should know by now that it kills. So I'm not going to remind you about the 440,000 Americans who die each year from smoking-related diseases or the almost 9 million who develop at least one serious illness from it (for further details and statistics, check out the following link: http://www.cdc.gov/tobacco/data_statistics/fact_sheets/fast_facts/#use).

I shouldn't even mention that with an average price of $5.50 per pack, a smoker who goes through twenty cigarettes a day will puff away a cool $2000 of their hard-earned cash every year. But there are no nagging judgments coming from me.

After all, smoking is a choice, right? Just like taking cocaine, giving an eight-year-old a loaded pistol and teaching them to shoot, or playing chicken across a busy freeway.

The same goes for booze. Though *usually* not as harmful as smoking, alcohol too has numerous and potentially fatal health risks associated with it. These risks can include cirrhosis of the liver, various cancers, and serious dependency issues. It's also expensive. At least limit your drinking, and try to think of it as more of a treat than an essential beverage.

Save Your Loose Change

Rather than throwing it onto the dining room table and before it all disappears down the back of your couch, drop your loose change into a coin bank. Before you know it, you will have saved yourself a surprising amount of money.

What you use as a bank is up to you. It could be a good old piggy bank, or a more modern bank with a flashy counter. However, sealable container will do. You can use a large jar with a slot cut into the lid or an old bottle with a mouth wide enough to put the money in.

I wouldn't bother with "novelty" banks, though, as they often cost a lot to buy in the first place and some even need expensive batteries to work properly (which pretty much defeats the purpose).

Swap Auto-Spending for Auto-Saving

Keep the number of direct debits and monthly subscriptions you possess to an absolute minimum. The only exception should be if you're able to get better service deals by using them. For example, some utility suppliers and cable networks often have preferential rates for customers with direct debit subscriptions. Instead, ask your bank about signing up for a direct deposit or automatic savings program.

Keep Your Money Moving

Keep an eye on the bank rates, and transfer your savings each time you find one with a better return. If you find you're not touching the majority of your savings after three or four months, then move it into a higher interest account at the best bank you can find.

Some Simple Tips for Budgeting Your Income

Not having a budget is like running through a darkened maze blindfolded. You'll have no real idea what you can afford, how much you need to live on, or how much you're wasting. Even worse, you'll be practically inviting debt into your life and you won't be able to save much of anything!

The good news is that budgeting is pretty straightforward if you keep on top of it. There are also plenty of tools out there to help you. Below are some simple pieces of advice to help you create a budget and take control of your spending.

1) Determine Your Income

If you receive a regular wage, figuring out your income is a synch to do. But, if you're self-employed, you'll need to average your earnings over the past 6 months or so, then deduct a 10% "safety margin" from that to give you a ballpark figure to work with. Remember to only consider your net income, not your gross income (the money BEFORE tax has been taken out).

2) Determine Your Regular Outgoing Spending

Now comes the worrisome part; thinking about what you regularly spend each month! It usually helps to write this all down. Using a spreadsheet or good old-fashioned pencil and paper, create a list of **"essential"** and **"non-essential"** spending.

The essential list should include all the things you spend to maintain a *basic* standard of living. This would include things such as food, water, utilities, mortgage payments, rent, etc. Everything else goes on the non-essential list.

Always bear in mind that the items on the essential list MUST be paid, so the money for them will NOT be available for entries on the non-essential list. Therefore, you need to be VERY honest with yourself and *get your priorities straight.* Are your cosmetics *really* an essential in comparison to your mortgage? Is the cable television really as vital to you as your car?

3) Calculate What's Available and Prioritize Those Cuts!

Get a grand total of everything from the two lists of essential and non-essential expenditures and deduct the result from your total income. If you end up with a positive number, than you're doing okay. If the result is negative, you're living beyond your means. If that's the case, it's time to get a better job, tighten that belt, or sell off a body part. If you're in this situation, NEVER cut back on the essentials, while you still have things you can do without. Instead, grab that non-essentials list, prioritize it, and start cutting back on the items from the bottom of that list.

If you're lucky enough to have a little extra money at the end of the month, split the excess cash across an **emergency fund** (about 10%) to pay for any unexpected expenditures, a **savings budget**, which you won't plan to touch (set aside as much as you can), and a **spending budget** which you can use to splurge on life's little luxuries! Always abide by the criterion of these budgets and don't be tempted to dip into the savings budget or emergency fund. If your spending budget is too small for want you want, just shrug your shoulders, and do without!

Setting Budget and Financial Goals

Think about what you want to achieve by setting short and long-term goals. Short-term goals could include limiting the amount you spend or saving a few hundred dollars every month. Long-term goals should include things such as being able to put down a deposit for a mortgage, saving for a vacation, or buying a new car. Make sure you have something to be working towards to help you stay on track with your budget!

Checkout Budgeting Software

Any old spreadsheet application will do, but many personal finance suites like Quicken or Microsoft Money have built-in tools that can help you to produce a customized budget. These are costly solutions, however, and there are some great websites out there (such as mint.com) that offer a similar service for free!

Emergency! Tips to Make Money Fast When You're Completely Broke

This chapter is for those who are really in a dire situation and have suddenly or unexpectedly found themselves out of work. If that wasn't bad enough, finding out you haven't made adequate financial provisions to support yourself during this period can be catastrophic. The result is you literally falling off the money ladder with a loud bump. Ouch!

This can leave you desperately wondering where and when the next paycheck will be coming from, but all is not lost. Hopefully, I can show you some quick ways to instantly reverse this situation – maybe even by tomorrow – so you can begin to see some of those lovely bucks once again!

The Right Mindset

The very first thing you must do is to get into the right mindset and start thinking positively about your situation. This might not sound very easy. But, whatever you do, you don't want to panic. Focusing on the "solution" instead of the "problem" is paramount to achieving this.

You might not realize it, but there are many potential customers out there who are desperate for small jobs to be done and services to be provided AND they're ready to pay *you* to do them! This information is something you can maximize and use to your benefit.

With the correct mindset, you'll be the one in "control" and you can soon be earning money again. But before we go any further, let's do some serious damage control and begin plugging any holes in your money ship before it sinks any further.

Plugging the Holes to Stop Your Money Leaks

As I've already mentioned, what's really important is to implement damage control, and that means limiting the amount of money you're currently spending. Remember, this is only a temporary measure, but it'll go a long way in helping to keep you afloat!

The first thing to do is to visit the relevant agencies in your area to find out if they can help with your rent payment, electric bill, or even provide some food. Good places to begin with are the Salvation Army, food pantries, or local government agencies.

Don't forget that you may also need to temporarily change your lifestyle and personal habits. You should start thinking about how much you're spending on food by cutting out the junk food and starting to eat cheap and healthily. Your health is going to be the key to your wealth when climbing the money ladder and this is especially true when putting your foot on the first rung. So what comes next?

Give Me a Job

You're probably thinking this is the most obvious solution, and you're right. However, you may think that getting a new job takes time, so you won't be receiving that much-needed paycheck for a while. Wrong – you can get a job right away and here's how to do it.

The first place to start is with your family and friends. Ask them for help, not handouts. Offer to do odd jobs for them for cash. These jobs can range from mowing the lawn, to decorating a room, to cleaning the back yard. You'll be surprised at how quickly you can find some temporary work.

The next place to find some quick cash-in-hand work is on Craigslist. Look under the section for your local area to see if anyone has any jobs that need to be done. If you look under the domestic category, you can find such jobs as babysitting, pet sitting, or house cleaning. With these types of jobs, you'll often find that if you're good and reliable other people will be promoting you through word-of-mouth and contacting you to do the same for them.

Other good places to try are USFreeAds or if you're in Canada, Kijiji. Other quick cash-in-hand jobs might involve handing out flyers or holding a billboard in a shopping center. Don't feel that you're belittling yourself by doing these jobs because they're all quick, short-term solutions for putting dollars into your empty pockets.

You won't be alone and many famous faces have been in this situation too. In fact, Michael Dell, the founder and CEO of Dell computers, washed dishes in a Chinese restaurant, while multi-millionaire business tycoon Donald Trump started by collecting soda bottles and turning them in for the deposit money. With this in mind, you can now start climbing that money ladder to reach bigger and better things.

Offering a Service

Okay, you've done a bit of work here and there, and you've now earned some cash. Now you can ramp things up and really start to bring in the money. The easiest way to do this is to provide a service. Don't worry because anyone can do this! You don't need to be an expert carpenter, plumber, or music teacher (although it would obviously be helpful if you were). Here are a few tried and tested ideas.

I've already mentioned that "health is wealth" and this is where it becomes especially important. Offering labor or services is always in huge demand. Many people in your neighborhood are probably looking for window cleaning services, snow shoveling, or even someone to clean up the backyard.

Remember that *the more unappealing the work is to others, the more opportunity there is for you.* A case in point would be cleaning up dog poop from someone's backyard. As long as you have a strong stomach, that could be a good starting job. However, there are several less smelly ideas below (and I'm sure you can think of many others yourself).

Do you have a drill? If so, you could provide peephole installation. This involves drilling a small hole through someone's front door and installing a peephole so the occupant can see who is standing outside. The cheapest ones can be bought for only about $2, but you can easily charge $20-25 for the installation. Can you imagine how much you could earn if you just installed a few of these each day?

Another way to earn some fast money is by offering to paint people's house numbers on the curb outside the front of their home. The going rate for this is about $10. Again, this could soon add up to a lot if you do it throughout the course of the day.

How about buying a bucket and sponge and visiting the local car dealers? Offer to clean all their cars. You'll be surprised with how much you can earn from this.

If working outside isn't for you, how about visiting all the bars in your area and offering to work "cash in hand" as a substitute when any of their staff can't come in or as an extra person when they are particularly busy? This can be especially productive during the holiday seasons.

Providing all of these services would most likely result in recurring work while you wait to get back into full-time employment. You never know, maybe these could lead to a permanent position or even to owning your own full-time business. But whatever the results, you'll find that you have moved up the money ladder.

These services can all be advertised in classifieds online, local bulletin boards, or if you can afford it, using printed handouts or flyers. There's one thing to remember when distributing flyers: don't put them into peoples' mailboxes as that's illegal. What you must do is hang them from the doorknobs, or alternatively, put them on the windshield of their cars.

Selling Things

Do you have any unwanted items you could sell? If the answer is "yes," then now is the time to do so. Obviously, the first place to sell them is on eBay, followed by Craigslist. But, what if you have nothing to sell? What should you do? Don't worry – there's a solution!

Go to The Freecycle Network and join your local group. Once there, you can browse the items and choose the ones you'll be able to sell via the classified ads, eBay, or Craigslist. You simply arrange a collection time with the owners and pick up the goods! Remember, not to tell them that you plan to resell their items. Freecycle is specifically intended for recycling. This may seem a little dishonest, but your personal needs must take precedence when you're strapped for cash!

A Win-Win Situation

If you feel like you've hit rock-bottom because you're in dire need of some money, then hopefully this chapter will have shown you that there's light at the end of the tunnel – a tunnel that is, in fact, not very long. Because of the Internet, climbing back onto the financial ladder has never been easier. Even though it might take a little extra confidence and require making some uncomfortable decisions, it's a win-win situation for everyone. Customers and clients will appreciate your efforts, and more importantly, you'll once again be putting cash back into your pocket – fast!

About the Author

Judith Turnbridge is a married artist with an interest in interior design. She enjoys painting, calligraphy, and caring for her garden. Her two children have now grown up and flown the nest and the two hungry mouths she now feeds belong to her two fluffy cats.

Other books by Judith Turnbridge:

Super Simple Home Cleaning: The Best House Cleaning Tips for Green Cleaning the Home

The Super Simple 30-Day Home Cleaning Plan: Making Time to Beat the Grime

How to Organize Your Life to Maximize Your Day: Effective Time Management Tips and Ideas to Simplify Your Life

How to Declutter Your Home for Simple Living: Decluttering Tips and Closet Organization Ideas for Creating Your Own Personal Oasis

Out of Sight, Out of Mind: Easy Home Organization Tips and Storage Solutions for Clutter-Free Living

Nature's Miracle Elixir: The Essential Health Benefits of Coconut Oil

How to Survive a Disaster: Emergency Preparedness for You and Your Family

Printed in Poland
by Amazon Fulfillment
Poland Sp. z o.o., Wrocław